machine embroidered
napkin wraps
and table linens

SNEZ BABIC • JANICE WRAY

INCLUDES CD

43 Embroidery designs All the designs you need to make the projects in this book.
6 Bonus projects Step-by-step instructions for 6 complete projects.
Creative combinations Embroidery layout ideas for inspired table tops.
Embroidery specifications Design information for stitching success.

TRAFFORD
PUBLISHING™

GET THE MOST OUT OF THIS BOOK AND EMBROIDERY DESIGN CD

The projects and designs in *Machine Embroidered Napkin Wraps and Table Linens* require the use of a computerized sewing machine with hooped embroidery capabilities using preprogrammed embroidery designs. Software may or may not be essential, depending on the nature of your machine.

Your machine must be able to accept one of the following embroidery formats: .hus, .shv, .vp3, .pes, .xxx and .dst. You must have the software/hardware capability to transfer the embroidery designs from the CD to your machine, for stitching out. To stitch the napkin wraps, your embroidery field must be at least 6" x 9 1/2". All other designs will fit in a 4" x 4" embroidery field. You must also have a good working knowledge of your embroidery sewing machine and software.

We assume you know how to access the contents of a CD. Some of the documents on the enclosed CD are in Adobe® PDF format, therefore you will require Adobe® Reader® to view them. Adobe® Reader® software can be downloaded from the www.adobe.com web site.

While every effort is taken to ensure the accuracy of the information and content presented in this publication and enclosed CD, we cannot accept responsibility for typographical errors or misinterpretation of information.

Note for Librarians: A cataloguing record for this book is available from Library and Archives Canada at www.collectionscanada. ca/amicus/index-e.html
ISBN 1-4251-1077-0

Printed in Victoria, BC, Canada. Printed on paper with minimum 30% recycled fibre.
Trafford's print shop runs on "green energy" from solar, wind and other environmentally-friendly power sources.

Offices in Canada, USA, Ireland and UK

Book sales for North America and international:
Trafford Publishing, 6E–2333 Government St.,
Victoria, BC V8T 4P4 CANADA
phone 250 383 6864 (toll-free 1 888 232 4444)
fax 250 383 6804; email to orders@trafford.com
Book sales in Europe:
Trafford Publishing (uk) Limited, 9 Park End Street, 2nd Floor
Oxford, UK OX1 1HH United Kingdom
phone +44 (0)1865 722 113 (local rate 0845 230 9601)
facsimile +44 (0)1865 722 868; info.uk@trafford.com
Order online at:
trafford.com/06-2836

10 9 8 7 6 5 4 3 2

machine embroidered napkin wraps and table linens

This book is designed to help you imagine, plan and create beautiful embroidered napkin wraps and coordinating table linens for your home using your embroidery sewing machine and the embroidery designs on the enclosed CD.

The first part of the book pictures a series of table linen project themes for favorite seasonal, holiday, and lifetime events. Each theme features an embroidered Napkin Wrap design, made entirely in the machine embroidery hoop. Every Napkin Wrap is accompanied by coordinating table linens in a variety of styles and shapes and embroidered with designs ranging from a single exquisite motif to multiple arrangements of simple classics. You will also see special embroidery techniques such as cutwork, eyelet and appliqué, along with a selection of edge finishes; from simple folded hems to beautiful satin scalloped edges. Use the ideas in this book to plan your own table linen projects. You can make table linens just as they are shown, or design your own using the information outlined in the 2nd part of the book. Take note of the elegant charger plate and whimsical table banner projects - the enclosed CD contains bonus instructions for these unique table top solutions.

You will find the napkin wrap embroidery design files and their coordinating design files on the enclosed CD. See page 36 for the CD and more information. We suggest you open the read_me.txt file first to familiarize yourself with the CD contents. We hope you find *Machine Embroidered Napkin Wraps and Table Linens* a helpful and inspiring resource for making table linens of all types, all year round.

Snez & Janice

contents

Violets & Eyelets

Napkin Wrap Follow directions on page 18 using embroidery design 700d01_01. Shown customized before stitching.

Charger Plate Follow Bonus instructions on enclosed CD using designs 700d01_02 and eyelet embroidery design 700d14_01. See filename: 700d_violets_eyelets.pdf.

Wedding Bells

Napkin Wrap Follow directions on page 18 using cutwork embroidery design 700d09_01. Shown customized before stitching.

Centerpiece Follow Bonus instructions on enclosed CD using cutwork embroidery 700d09_02 and eyelet embroidery design 700d14_01. See filename: 700d_wedding_bells.pdf.

Eyelets & Daisies

Napkin Wrap Follow directions on page 18 using eyelet embroidery design 700d03_01.

Charger Plate Follow Bonus instructions on enclosed CD using eyelet embroidery designs 700d03_02 and 700d03_03. See filename: 700d_eyelets_daisies.pdf.

Candlewick Evening
(at right)

Napkin Wrap Follow directions on page 18 using design 700d02_01.
Shown customized before stitching.

Charger Plate Follow Bonus instructions on enclosed CD using designs
700d02_02 and 700d02_03. See filename: 700d_candlewick.pdf.

Easter Treats

Napkin Wrap Follow directions on page 18 using appliqué embroidery design 700d11_01.

Centerpiece Features appliqué embroidery design 700d11_02 and hemstitched hem finish.

Springtime Blooms
(at right)

Napkin Wrap Follow directions on page 18 using design 700d06_01.

Table Topper Features design 700d06_02 and hemstitched hem finish.

Company Picnic
(at left)

Napkin Wrap Follow directions on page 18 using design 700d05_01. Shown customized before stitching.

Napkin Features design 700d05_02 with topstitched hem finish.

Table Banner Follow Bonus instructions on enclosed CD using design 700d05_04. See filename: 700d_table_banners.pdf.

Citrus & Sunshine
Napkin Wrap Follow directions on page 18 using design 700d04_01.

Placemat Features design 700d04_04 and satin stitched hem finish.

Table Topper Features design 700d04_02 and satin stitched hem finish.

11

Halloween Helpline

Napkin Wrap Follow directions on page 18 using design 700d12_01.

Cocktail Napkin Features design 700d12_02 and fringed hem finish.

Table Banner Follow Bonus instructions on enclosed CD using design 700d12_03.
See filename: 700d_table_banners.pdf.

A Casual Thanksgiving

Napkin Wrap Follow directions on page 18 using design 700d13_01.

Coaster Features design 700d13_02 with topstitched hem finish.

Charger Plate Follow Bonus instructions on enclosed CD using designs 700d13_02, 03 and 04.
See filename: 700d_casual_thanksgiving.pdf.

14

Oak & Acorns

(at left)

Napkin Wrap Follow directions on page 18 using design 700d07_01.

Placemat Features design 700d07_03 and topstitched hem finish.

Tablecloth Features design 700d07_02 with topstitched hem finish.

Holly for the Holidays

Napkin Wrap Follow directions on page 18 using design 700d10_01.

Placmat Features design 700d10_02 with topstitched hem finish.

Tablecloth Features designs 700d10_02 and 04 with topstitched hem finish.

Big Boy Birthday

Napkin Wrap Follow directions on page 18 using design 700d08_01.
Shown customized before stitching.

Coaster Features design 700d08_02 and topstitched hem finish.

Table Banner Follow Bonus instructions on enclosed CD using design 700d08_02 and 03.
See filename: 700d_table_banners.pdf.

Table Runner Features satin stitched hem finish.

EMBROIDERED NAPKIN WRAPS

These decorative napkin wraps are pretty, practical and easy to make - entirely in your embroidery hoop! We've included styles to suit a variety of themes. Whether it is for a casual luncheon, an elegant dinner party or a holiday celebration, there's sure to be one to suit every occasion.

Choose a napkin wrap from those shown on pages 4 to 16. The embroidery design files for the napkin wraps are included on the enclosed CD. For help finding the files, see the read_me.txt on the CD. Follow the instructions on the following pages to embroider the napkin wraps.

Tip Some of our napkin wraps serve double duty, acting as both napkin wrap and place card. Before stitching, use the lettering from your embroidery software to insert a name, initials and/or a date in the spaces provided on some of the napkin wraps. If you do not own embroidery software with lettering, use the built-in lettering on your embroidery sewing machine after the napkin wraps are embroidered.

napkin wraps embroidery

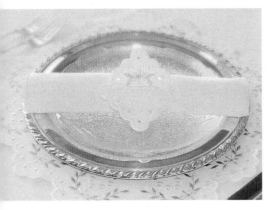

For 8 napkin wraps:
A napkin wrap embroidery design
from the enclosed CD

14" x 45" strip of linen or cotton/linen
blend

40wt rayon thread in desired colors

Embroidery bobbin thread

Stabilizer: Wash away for eyelet and
cutwork napkin wrap, Tear away for
all others.

Temporary adhesive spray

Seam sealant

Spray on starch

4" curved embroidery scissors

*and for the eyelet napkin wrap
(700d03_01):*
Eyelet Cutter

*and for the appliqué napkin wrap
(700d11_01):*
One 3"x 4" strip of cotton print

1. Pre wash the linen or cotton/linen blend to preshrink. While still damp, spray with starch, let dry slightly and press. Be sure to use a press cloth as starched fabrics scorch easily.

2. Setup your sewing machine for embroidery following manufacturer's directions. Thread on top with the rayon and the embroidery bobbin thread in the bobbin.

3. Spray the wrong side of the fabric with the temporary adhesive spray. Adhere onto the stabilizer. Starting at one end of the fabric, hoop fabric and stabilizer. Put hoop into position onto your embroidery sewing machine.

4. Stitch napkin wraps using one of the following methods:

For the eyelet napkin wrap (#700d03_01) a. Begin stitching the design. When your embroidery sewing machine stops for the color change and the eyelets have been outlined, remove the hoop from your embroidery sewing machine but *do not remove the fabric from the hoop.* With your eyelet cutter, cut out the fabric in the eyelets.

b. Return the hoop to your embroidery sewing machine and stitch the next color. A satin stitch covers the eyelets. Finish stitching the embroidery design, changing thread colors as desired.

c. Stitch out 7 more napkin wraps to complete the set of 8. Trim away all thread tails from the front and the back of each napkin wrap. Hold under running water to remove the wash away stabilizer. Wash, rinse and dry. While still damp, spray with starch, let dry slightly and press.

Go to "Finishing" on page 20.

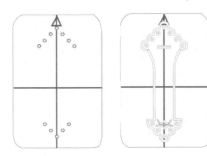

For the cutwork napkin wrap (#700d09_01) a. Stitch out the first color in the design. This outlines the cutwork area. A color stop will stop your embroidery sewing machine. Do not change thread color. The color stop is inserted only to allow you to cut out the fabric inside the cutwork areas.

b. When the stitching stops, remove the hoop from your embroidery sewing machine, but *do not remove the fabric from the hoop.* Trim the fabric layer only, inside and close to the straight stitching outline but *do not trim the wash away stabilizer.* A pair of quality 4″ curved embroidery scissors is essential.

c. Put the hoop back into position onto your embroidery sewing machine and continue stitching. Richelieu bars are stitched in the cutout area. A satin stitch outline is stitched to cover the raw edges. Finally, the remainder of the design stitches out.

d. Stitch out 7 more napkin wraps to complete the set of 8. Trim away all thread tails from the front and the back of each napkin wrap. Hold under running water to remove the wash away stabilizer. Wash, rinse and dry. While still damp, spray with starch, let dry slightly and press.

Go to "Finishing" on page 20.

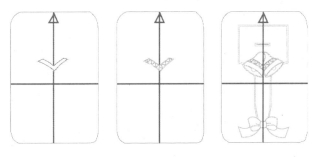

For the appliqué napkin wrap (#700d11_01) a. Stitch out the first color in the design. This marks out the appliqué area with a straight stitch. A color stop will stop your embroidery sewing machine. Do not change thread color. The color stop is inserted only to allow you to place the appliqué fabric into position in the embroidery hoop.

b. Spray the back of the cotton strip with the temporary adhesive spray and place over the marked out areas on the ends of the egg shape.

c. Stitch the next color. This outlines the shape and holds the appliqué fabric in place with a straight stitch. A color stop will stop your embroidery sewing machine. Do not change thread color. The color stop is inserted only to allow you to trim away the excess appliqué fabric.

d. Once the stitching stops, remove the hoop from your embroidery sewing machine but **do not remove the fabric from the hoop.** Trim away the excess fabric close to the straight stitching outline.

e. Put the hoop back into position onto your embroidery sewing machine and stitch out the next color. A satin stitch outlines the appliqué, covering the raw edge. Stitch out the remaining colors to complete the napkin wrap.

f. Stitch out 7 more napkin wraps to complete the set of 8. Trim away all thread tails from the front and the back of each napkin wrap. Leave the tear away stabilizer in place for support, as desired.

Go to "Finishing" below.

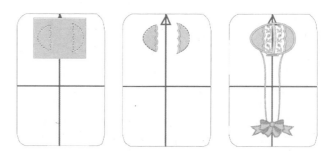

For all other napkin wraps Stitch out the napkin wrap design and then stitch out 7 more to complete the set of 8. Trim away all thread tails from the front and the back of each napkin wrap. Leave the tear away stabilizer in place for support, as desired.

Finishing 5. From the wrong side, dab seam sealant along the outer edge of each napkin wrap. Also dab a bit of seam sealant down the center of the buttonholes. Let dry completely. Cut out each napkin wrap, trimming close to the satin stitching. Cut buttonholes open.

6. Tuck the lower end of the napkin wrap through the buttonhole. You will have to scrunch up or fold the end to make it fit through the buttonhole. Press the napkin wrap as necessary. Slip a napkin through the ring of the napkin wrap.

EMBROIDERED TABLE LINENS

There's no denying that once we have an exciting embroidery project in mind, we are anxious to get to the fun part - stitching the beautiful embroideries we have chosen. However, whether it is a tablecloth, placemat, table runner, or a tiny little coaster, the more carefully you plan your design, the more successful your project will be. Follow these steps to design and create custom embroidered linens for your table.

Choose your project To plan your project accurately, you will need to have an idea of its finished size. Go to *made to measure* on page 22 to determine a desired finished size for your project. You will probably find that as you plan your project, you'll need to adjust the finished size to adapt your embroidery layout plan or vice versa. Therefore, think of this only as a *working* size until your design plan is finalized.

Plan your project You will need to decide how you want to arrange the embroidery design(s) you have chosen. Perhaps you will embroider an edging all around, using one or more of the edging designs that are on the enclosed CD. Or perhaps you will choose to embroider one exquisite, perfectly placed design. Whether your embroidery is elaborate or simple, planning is always important. Go to *embroidery placement planning* on page 23 to begin planning your embroidery project. If your project does not have an embroidered edging, you will need to plan for a hem or decorative edge finish. Go to *hems and decorative edges* on page 26 to plan for this. Lastly, go to *finalize your project plan* on page 29.

Create your project All your careful planning will prove well worthwhile as you confidently mark and cut your fabric and then easily stitch out your embroideries. Go to *table linens embroidery* on page 30 to begin creating your project. If you are using an embroidery design from the enclosed CD that features eyelet, cutwork or applique, refer to *special embroidery techniques* on page 32 to be sure you are stitching these designs out correctly. The final step to creating your project is to finish the hems and edges as planned. To refresh your knowledge, go back to *hems and decorative edges* on page 26.

For some embroidery layout ideas Go to the Creative Combination PDF file on the enclosed CD (filename:700d_creative_combos.pdf). It is packed with fabulous and fascinating ideas for combining and arranging the embroidery designs used in this book. And remember, if you own embroidery software you may be able to customize your entire design grouping or parts of it.

made to measure

Follow the guidelines below to decide on the desired finished measurement for your table linen style. Don't add hems or embroidery hoop allowances yet - you will determine this later, as your design plan progresses. This is because your finished size may need to change to adapt to that "must have" embroidery layout idea that you are dreaming of. Use these guidelines only as a starting point and then proceed to *embroidery placement planning* on the next page to begin working on your design plan.

TABLECLOTH

To determine the finished size of your tablecloth measure the length and width of the tabletop and then add the drop. The tablecloth should just brush your legs while you are seated. This means that the drop for most tables is approximately 10" to 12", depending on the height of the table and chairs. To measure the drop, sit down at your table and measure from the edge of the tabletop to the top of your legs.

Finished size =
(tabletop length + 2 drops) x (tabletop width + 2 drops)

If table is oval or has curved edges: you can curve the fabric to match. Place a sheet of paper over the curve of the table and either crease the paper along the curve or trace with a pencil. Use this paper pattern to curve the tablecloth to size. For perfectly round tables, calculate the circle as follows.

Finished size = (tabletop diameter + 2 drops)

TABLE RUNNER

Table runners generally measure anywhere from 14" to 16" in width and can be almost any length, depending on their purpose. For example, decorative runners usually sit in the center of the table, so they should measure approximately 2/3 of the tabletop length. For a tabletop that measures 60" in length, the finished length of the table runner would be 40".

The length of table runners that hang over the edge of the table can be calculated exactly as for a tablecloth.

Finished size = tabletop length + 2 drops

CENTERPIECE OR DOILY

These are strictly decorative, placed under candy dishes, vases, bowls, etc. Size is entirely as desired.

PLACEMAT

Placemats generally measure 12" x 18" to 14" x 20" depending on the size of your intended place setting. To choose the right size, draw two rectangles onto a sheet of paper, 12" x 18" and 14" x 20". Arrange a place setting onto the paper over the rectangles and select the size that best fits your place setting.

CHARGER PLATE

Charger plates measure 14" to 16", depending on the size of your intended place setting. They can be round or square. To choose the right size, draw two squares or circles onto a sheet of paper, 14" and 16". Arrange a place setting onto the paper over the shapes and select the size that best suits.

NAPKIN

Napkins generally measure 16", 18", 20" or 22" square. The more formal the occasion, the larger the napkin.

COCKTAIL NAPKIN

Cocktail napkins generally measure 5" to 8" square, as desired.

COASTER

Coasters measure approximately 4" across, round or square, as desired.

TABLE BANNER

Our table banner is a fun new project that is embroidered with a seasonal motif or message. It sits on top of a table runner, tablecloth or even a bare table. The table banner measures 3" in width and is whatever length you desire. You will find complete directions for table banners on the enclosed CD. Look for filename: 700d_table_banners.pdf.

embroidery placement planning

Whether you choose to embroider a little or a lot, the key to success is planning. There are no hard and fast rules but there are many things to consider when planning an embroidered project: the size of the design, project, number of designs, and time and materials restraints. Ultimately, you will have to rely on your own taste and common sense.

Embroidery placement templates are our favorite tool for positioning embroideries accurately. Follow one of the methods outlined below and the directions on the following pages to plan perfectly placed embroideries using embroidery placement templates.

For a single design placement Print or stitch out an embroidery placement template for the design you will be using as described on the next page. Your project will need a hem or decorative edge finish. After you make your template, go to *hems and decorative edges* on page 26.

For embroidered edgings and more elaborate design arrangements Print or stitch out embroidery placement templates for each of the designs you will be using as described on the next page. Use the templates to make a Paper Placement Layout as described on page 25, to plan your design layout. Once your design plan is established on paper, you will transfer the markings from the paper to your fabric. If your project requires it, go to *hems and decorative edges* on page 26. Otherwise, proceed to *finalize your project plan* on page 29 to prepare your project plan for embroidery.

Tip If you own embroidery software you may be able to customize entire design groupings or parts of it with the software. Consult your software manual for more information.

EMBROIDERY PLACEMENT TEMPLATES

Embroidery placement templates are key to positioning embroideries accurately. There are 2 types of embroidery placement templates, printed and stitched. The one you choose depends on your resources and requirements.

Printed embroidery placement templates

Making a paper template is a good idea if you are making more than one of any item, as marking multiple items will be easier and more consistent. Many embroidery software programs will allow you to print out an image of your embroidery design. To be used as a template, the printed image must be 100% actual size. It must accurately show the horizontal and vertical centerlines of the embroidery area and the embroidery as it is positioned to stitch out.

To make a printed embroidery placement template: Print an image of the embroidery design. Make sure it meets the requirements outlined above. Position the inner embroidery hoop over the image, matching up the horizontal and vertical centerlines on the image with the markings on the inner hoop. Trace along the inside edge of the hoop. Cut out the template around the traced line. You now have a template for perfect positioning.

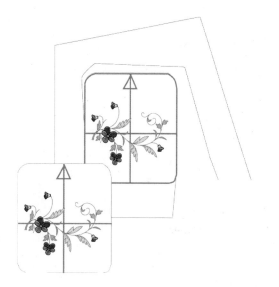

Stitched embroidery placement templates

If you do not own an embroidery software program that can print an image of a design suitable for use as a placement template, you can stitch out an actual sample of the design. In fact, sometimes stitching a sample design is preferable to printing its image. Stitching the design gives you an opportunity to ensure that your thread color(s) work, that the stabilizer supports the fabric and design properly and that the design stitches out as expected. It is also a good way to familiarize yourself with special embroidery techniques such as eyelet, cutwork and appliqué.

To make a stitched embroidery placement template: Setup your sewing machine for embroidery following your manufacturer's directions. Thread with rayon thread on top and embroidery bobbin thread in the bobbin. Cut a strip of cotton and a matching strip of tear away stabilizer - these need to be just large enough to hoop comfortably. Hoop fabric and stabilizer. With a marking pencil, draw a line down the vertical center and the horizontal center of your hoop. Trace along the inside edge of the hoop. Place the hoop into position on your embroidery sewing machine and stitch out the design. Remove hoop from machine and remove fabric from hoop. Cut around the traced line. You now have a template for perfect placement. If you need more than one template of the same design to plan your layout, simply make photocopies of the stitch out.

Tip Print your templates onto transparency film, so the designs can be seen from both sides. When a clear template is flipped over from side to side, you see the mirror image. This eliminates the need to print mirror images of designs. Store your templates carefully for future use.

PAPER PLACEMENT LAYOUTS

1. If your embroidery software program allows, print out a placement template for each embroidery design that you plan to use in your project, following directions on page 24. Print out as many copies of each design that you need. Refer to the **Tip** at the bottom of this page.

If you cannot print out a template, make a stitched template following directions on page 24, and then make photocopies of the stitch outs as necessary.

2. Start with a sheet of paper that is 3″ to 4″ larger than the desired finished size of your project. Mark out the finished size or shape of your project onto the sheet of paper.

For help in determining the finished size of your table linen project, see "made to measure" on page 22.

Mark the horizontal and vertical centerlines. Mark a line at a 45-degree angle from each corner to divide the corner areas in half. Add additional markings as necessary to help with design placement.

3. To plan interior designs, move the placement templates around the area you wish to embroider, to find the most pleasing arrangements, using the marked lines as guides to balance the designs. Don't hesitate to adjust the size of your project to accommodate the pattern you wish to achieve. You can also overlap designs or space them slightly to achieve the desired effect.

4. To plan embroidered edgings, start along the center vertical or horizontal line and use the placement templates to measure out the number of repeats that you require to cover the edges. Be prepared to adjust

the size of your project slightly to accommodate the embroidery designs. For example, we planned to make a placemat with a finished size of 12″ x 18″. We measured out eyelet edging designs (700d14_01 and 02) all the way around, similar to the Eyelet Charger project on page 6. When we finished, we found that the placemat now measured 13 3/4″ x 19 1/4″. We adjusted our finished size to this new measurement.

5. Once you have the designs arranged as desired, transfer the centerlines, the orientation arrow and the starting points from the templates onto the paper. Mark a mirror symbol if the design needs to be mirrored from side to side.

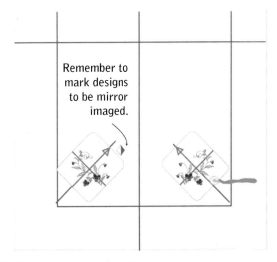

Remember to mark designs to be mirror imaged.

Tip For symmetrical design placement mark out one quarter of the project or one repeat of the pattern layout. For asymmetrical design placement you will need to mark out the entire project onto the paper.

You now have a paper pattern that shows you exactly where your embroideries will be placed. If your project requires one, go to *hems and decorative edges* on page 26. Otherwise, proceed to *finalize your project plan* on page 29 to prepare your project for embroidery.

hems and decorative edges

A hem or a decorative edge may be the last step in its construction, but it is an important consideration in the planning of a table linen project. Your choice will affect the look of the project and its intended use. For example, embroidered eyelet and scalloped satin edges add a sense of femininity, while a crisp topstitched edge adds tailored elegance to any table setting. Your choice will also affect the plan of the project, as you'll need to allow for hem allowances. Use the information on these pages to help you choose and plan for a hem or decorative edge that suits your style.

HEM WIDTHS

The minimal finished width of a hem is 1/2" for small items such as napkins and 3/4" for larger items such as tablecloths. The larger the piece, the wider you can make the hem. This is especially true on tablecloths, where wider hems add formality, for their added air of extravagance. Please note that wider hem allowances are more difficult to ease into curved pieces.

For the projects shown in this book We have chosen the narrowest of finished hem widths: 1/2" for small items such as napkins and 3/4" for larger items such as tablecloths. This allows us to embroider as close to a hemmed edge as we like, without interfering with the hem allowance.

HEMMING TECHNIQUES

Single fold hem Use this hem when your choice of finishing stitch serves to also finish the raw edge on the wrong side of the hem, such as satin stitched and hemstitched finishes. The single fold hem is a good choice for rounded shapes as the single layer makes it easier to ease in excess fabric. Because some hem finishing stitches are difficult to stitch in curves, it is a good idea to experiment on rounded corners and shapes.

With mitred corners (for straight edges and corners): With a fade away marker, mark a hem on all four sides. Mark a 45-degree line across the intersections in the corners as illustrated. Fold and press along the marked line on all sides, do not press in the corners. Following the diagrams first fold the corner along the 45-degree line. Fold the sides in as before and press. Stitch in place using the *satin stitched* or *hemstitched* method.

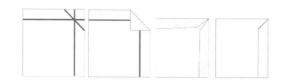

Without mitred corners (for curves): With a fade away marker, simply mark a hem all around. Fold and press along the marked line, easing in fullness. Stitch in place using the *satin stitched* or *hemstitched* method.

Please note: For this book, we've focussed on machine stitched hems and edges, rather than serged finishes. Sergers are great for quick and casual finishes to all your home linens. If you have a serger and would like to finish your embroidered table linens using one of the many available serged finishes, please consult your manufacturer's instructions.

Double fold hem Use this hem when your choice of finishing stitch does not serve to finish the raw edge on the wrong side of the hem, such as topstitching. The double fold hem is also a good choice when you want to create a crisp stable edge on both lightweight and heavier linen fabrics.

With mitred corners (for straight edges and corners): Mark two equally spaced hems on all four sides. Fold and press along the first line on all sides, do not press in the corners. Fold and press along the second line and again do not press in the corners. Following the diagrams, first fold the corner at point A to meet point B. Fold the corner again over the first fold, encasing points A and B. Fold the sides in as before and press. Stitch in place using the *topstitched* method.

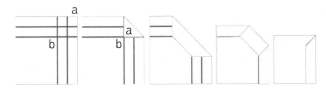

Without mitred corners (for curves): With a fade away marker, simply mark two equally spaced hems all around. You may choose to make the first hem width narrower to make easing in the excess fabric easier. Fold and press along the marked line, easing in fullness. Fold and press along the second line, again easing in fullness. Stitch in place using the *topstitched* method.

HEM FINISHES

Topstitched When you would rather bring attention to other details, use a simple straight stitch to secure the hem of your project in place.

To create a topstitched hem: Use the *double fold hem* technique to hem your project. Setup your sewing machine for regular sewing.

Thread on top and in the bobbin with matching cotton thread. Attach the regular presser foot. Select a straight stitch and set the length to 3mm. Topstitch the hem in place. Pivot at the corners as necessary. Press.

Satin stitched It is very likely that your embroidery sewing machine has a multitude of built-in decorative satin stitches that can add a decorative touch and unique look to your linens. Almost any one of them will work to topstitch the hem of your linens in place.

To create a satin stitched hem: Use the *single fold hem* technique to hem your project. Setup your sewing machine for regular sewing.

Thread with 40wt. rayon on top and embroidery bobbin thread in the bobbin. Attach a decorative presser foot or the open toe appliqué foot. Both these feet have a groove on the underside that allows the satin stitching to pass through freely and easily. Select the satin stitch of your choice.

Place a strip of tear away stabilizer underneath and topstitch the hem in place, just covering the raw edge of the hem with the satin stitch. Pivot at the corners as necessary. Remove the stabilizer and trim away any fraying thread from the hem. Press.

Hemstitched Create a traditional looking hemstitched edge using a wing needle and your machine's decorative stitches. The wing needle pushes the fabric threads apart to create tiny decorative holes in the fabric.

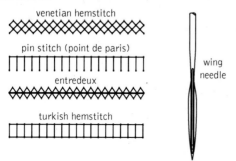

venetian hemstitch

pin stitch (point de paris)

entredeux

turkish hemstitch

wing needle

To create a hemstitched hem: Use the **single fold hem** technique on page 26 to hem your project. Setup your sewing machine for regular sewing. Thread on top and in the bobbin with heirloom cotton thread. Insert a wing needle and attach the regular presser foot. Select the hemstitch of your choice.

You may need to adjust the length and width of some hemstitches to achieve a desired look. Test on a scrap piece of your fabric first.

Place a strip of wash away stabilizer underneath and topstitch the hem in place, just catching the raw edge of the hem with the hemstitch. Pivot at the corners. Remove the stabilizer following manufacturer's directions. Trim away any fraying thread from the hem and press.

Fringed Fringed edges are one of the easiest finishes to create. They lend a casual feel to table linens. Make your fringe from 1/2″ up to 2″ wide. As a general rule, the larger your project, the wider the fringe can be. For the neatest fringes, cut your fabric absolutely on grain. Fringed edges are not a good choice for curved edges because the fringe will be uneven and bare in some areas.

Use a hemstitch such as the pin stitch (it looks like a heavy blanket stitch) and a wing needle. The wing needle pushes the fabric threads apart to create tiny decorative holes in the fabric. If you don't have a hemstitch on your machine, you can use a zig zag stitch instead and follow the directions given below.

To create a fringed edge: Mark the finished edge onto your project. Then mark a 2nd line outside the first, the desired width of your fringe. Trim along this line. Setup your sewing machine for regular sewing. Thread on top and in the bobbin with heirloom cotton thread. Insert the wing needle and attach the regular presser foot. Select the pin stitch hemstitch. Reduce the stitch length to 3mm and the width to 3.5mm.

Place a strip of wash away stabilizer underneath and topstitch along the first marked line. Stitch with the straight part of the pin stitch along the marked line and the zigzag part of the stitch into the fabric. Pivot at the corners. Remove the stabilizer. Pull away the threads to fringe the hem up to the stitching. Press.

finalize your project plan

Now that you have planned your embroidery layout and have decided on any needed hem finish, you are ready to calculate embroidery and/or hem allowances for your project. Add embroidery and/or hem allowances as given below and use the **Table Linen Calculator** below to add it all together. When you have checked your work, check it again and then go ahead and cut your fabric to size. Proceed to page 30 to embroider your project.

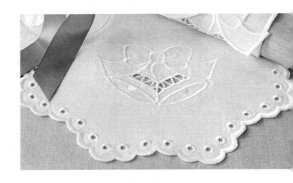

VERIFY THE PROJECT FINISHED MEASUREMENT

If you have had to adjust your finished measurement to allow for a more desirable embroidery placement or to adjust for embroidery design sizes, verify the new finished measurement of your project now. Refer to the section *made to measure* as necessary.

ADD EMBROIDERY HOOPING ALLOWANCE

If your project plan has an embroidered edge all around, such as the eyelet centerpiece shown here, add 3″ to 4″ hooping allowance around the edge of your finished project. If your project plan includes interior embroidery near finished edges, add 3″ to 4″ hooping allowance along the edges closest to the embroidery. Refer to the section *embroidery placement planning* as necessary.

The enclosed CD contains a copy of the Table Linen Calculator, which is larger than the one below. Find the file: 700d_calculator.pdf on your CD and print it out.

ADD HEM OR EDGE ALLOWANCE

Refer to the section *hems and decorative edges* as necessary, to add the following hem or edge allowance to your project plan.

For single fold hems Add the desired width of the hem on all sides. Our projects use the minimum of 3/4″ hem allowance for larger projects, such as table cloths and 1/2″ for smaller projects, such as napkins. Use this hem for *satin stitched* or *hemstitched* hem finishes.

For double fold hems Add twice the desired width of the hem on all sides. Our projects use the minimum of 1 1/2″ hem allowance for larger projects, such as table cloths and 1″ for smaller projects, such as napkins. Use this hem for *topstitched* hem finish.

For fringed edges Add the desired width of the fringe on all sides. Our projects use minimum of 3/4″ fringe allowance for larger projects such as table cloths and 1/2″ for smaller projects such as napkins. Use the *fringed edge* finish.

TABLE LINEN CALCULATOR

Please note: our calculator states minimum allowances. Add more if desired.

Table Linen Style	Final Finished Size Length x Width	plus Embroidery Hooping Allowance	plus Single Fold Hem Allowance	plus Double Fold Hem Allowance	plus Fringed Edging Allowance	plus Seam Allowance	= Total Cut Size Length x Width
Tablecloth	___ x ___	6″ (3″ per edge)	1 1/2″	3″	1 1/2″	N/A	___ x ___
Table Runner	___ x ___	6″ (3″ per edge)	1 1/2″	3″	1 1/2″	N/A	___ x ___
Centerpiece or Doily	___ x ___	6″ (3″ per edge)	1 1/2″	3″	1 1/2″	N/A	___ x ___
Placemat	___ x ___	6″ (3″ per edge)	1 1/2″	3″	1 1/2″	N/A	___ x ___
Charger	___ x ___	6″ (3″ per edge)	1 1/2″	3″	1 1/2″	N/A	___ x ___
Napkin	___ x ___	6″ (3″ per edge)	1″	2″	1″	N/A	___ x ___
Cocktail Napkin	___ x ___	6″ (3″ per edge)	1″	2″	1″	N/A	___ x ___
Coaster	___ x ___	6″ (3″ per edge)	1″	2″	1″	N/A	___ x ___
Table Banner	___ x ___	6″ (3″ per edge)	N/A	N/A	N/A	1/2″	___ x ___

table linens embroidery

Before you begin to embroider, have your project designed, measured and cut. Be sure you have prepared or added:
• Embroidery placement templates for each design (see page 24).
• A paper pattern layout, as required (see pages 23 to 25).
• Embroidery and/or hem allowances (see page 29).

You should also be aware of any special techniques such as eyelet, cutwork and appliqué that are used in the designs you are using. Designs with special stitching requirements are explained on pages 32 and 33.

Linen or cotton/linen blend fabric for your project

40wt rayon thread in desired colors

Embroidery bobbin thread

Tear away or wash away stabilizer

Temporary adhesive spray

Fade away marker

Seam sealant, for embroidered satin edges

SPECIAL TECHNIQUES

Some of the embroidery designs in this book are stitched out using special techniques. Before you begin, be sure you understand how these special embroidery designs are stitched out. See pages 32 and 33 for stitching information:

Eyelet Embroidery
700d03_02, 700d03_03
700d14_01, 700d14_02

Cutwork Embroidery
700d09_02

Appliqué Embroidery
700d11_02

1. Setup your sewing machine for embroidery following manufacturer's directions. Thread with the rayon on top and the embroidery bobbin thread in the bobbin.

2. Cut a strip of stabilizer to match your fabric. Spray the stabilizer with temporary adhesive spray and adhere onto the wrong side of the fabric.

3. Embroider your project using one of the following methods:

If you have prepared a paper pattern Transfer all markings from the paper pattern onto your fabric with a fade away marker. Be sure to include arrows and mirror symbols.

Stitch edging designs first: a. Starting at center, position the placement template onto the fabric, over a placement marking. Pin the template in place to hold. Hoop fabric and stabilizer matching the markings on the template with the markings on the inner hoop. Put hoop into position onto your embroidery sewing machine.

The edging designs featured in this book have been digitized in a way that allows you to easily line up repeats of the designs. It is important to position the designs correctly in the hoop so that they stitch out exactly as desired.

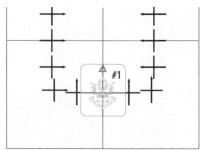

Before you begin stitching, please note that the very first stitch of the edging design is in the center of the hoop, then there is a jump stitch to the very start of the design at the left tip of the design. This is the *start point* that you will use to match up this and subsequent repeats of the design.

b. *You now need to advance to the **start point** of the design at the left edge without actually stitching: If your embroidery sewing machine allows you to advance stitch by stitch without actually stitching, use this function. Otherwise, you may have to do this manually, turning the flywheel towards you and without thread in the needle. Either way, this should only take a couple of stitches. Next, move the design within the hoop until the needle lines up with the **start point**. If this cannot be accomplished, you will need to re-hoop. Remove the template and stitch out the design.*

Position the placement template to the right of the design stitched, over the placement marking. Make sure that the left tip of the design touches the right tip of the design stitched. Pin the template into place to hold. Hoop fabric and stabilizer matching the markings on the template with the markings on the inner hoop. Put hoop into position onto your embroidery sewing machine. Follow from * to * to position and stitch out the design.

c. Repeat step b. until you have finished stitching all edging designs.

If you are finished embroidering, go to "Finishing" below.

Stitch interior designs next: Position the placement template onto the fabric, over a placement marking. Pin the template in place to hold. Hoop fabric and stabilizer matching the markings on the template with the markings on the inner hoop. Put hoop into position onto your embroidery sewing machine, remove the template and stitch out the design. Repeat as necessary to stitch out all the designs in your pattern.

Go to "Finishing" below.

If you do not have a paper pattern Position your placement template onto your fabric as desired. Pin the template in place to hold. Hoop fabric and stabilizer matching the markings on the template with the markings on the inner hoop. Put hoop into position onto your embroidery sewing machine, remove the template and stitch out the design.

Go to "Finishing" below.

Finishing 4. When you have finished all embroidery, trim away thread tails from the front and the back. Remove the stabilizer following manufacturer's direction. From the wrong side, dab seam sealant along any embroidered satin edges. Let dry and trim close to satin stitching.

5. Mark any remaining hem allowances once again, making sure the edges are straight and trim to size. Complete any remaining hems. Refer to directions on pages 26 to 28 for your chosen hem or edge finish.

special embroidery techniques

Some of the embroidery designs included on your CD feature special embroidery techniques and require special consideration when stitching. The method you use for stitching out any special design depends entirely on how they have been digitized. This section explains how to stitch out specific Eyelet, Cutwork and Appliqué designs that are included on the enclosed CD.

Our eyelet, cutwork and appliqué embroidery designs can be stitched onto many different types of fabrics, using a variety of threads. However, for best results with the eyelet and cutwork designs we recommend all natural fiber fabrics such as linen and cotton, 40wt rayon thread for the top, and embroidery bobbin thread for the bobbin.

Choose a wash away stabilizer for the eyelet and cutwork designs. It can be completely removed from your fabric, leaving a softer finish. Use either a single layer of medium or heavy weight wash away, or two layers of lightweight wash away.

1. Pre wash linen or cotton/blend fabrics to preshrink. While still damp, spray with starch, let dry slightly and press. Be sure to use a press cloth as starched fabrics scorch easily.

2. Setup your sewing machine for embroidery following manufacturer's directions. Thread with the rayon on top and embroidery bobbin thread in the bobbin.

3. Stitch embroidery using one of the following methods:

Designs 700d03_02, 700d03_03, 700d14_01 and 700d14_02 are eyelet embroidery designs. Follow the method below to stitch them out.

EYELET EMBROIDERY

a. Hoop fabric and stabilizer. Put hoop into position onto your embroidery sewing machine. Begin stitching the design. A color stop will stop your embroidery sewing machine. Do not change thread color. The color stop is inserted only to allow you to cut out the eyelets.

b. When your embroidery sewing machine stops for the color change and the eyelets have been outlined, remove the hoop from your embroidery sewing machine but *do not remove the fabric from the hoop*. With your eyelet cutter, cut out the fabric in the eyelets.

c. Return the hoop to your embroidery sewing machine and stitch the next color. A satin stitch covers the eyelets. Finish stitching the embroidery design, changing thread colors as desired.

d. When the design is complete, remove from hoop. Trim away all thread tails from the front and the back of the design. Hold under running water to remove the wash away stabilizer. Wash, rinse and dry. While still damp spray with starch, let dry slightly and press.

For eyelet embroidery,
you will also require an eyelet cutter and cutting mat
to cut out the holes in the eyelet area.

Design 700d09_02 is a cutwork embroidery design. Follow the method below to stitch it out.

Design 700d11_02 is an appliqué embroidery design. Follow the method below to stitch it out.

CUTWORK EMBROIDERY

a. Hoop fabric and wash away stabilizer. Put hoop into position onto your embroidery sewing machine. Stitch out the first color in the design. This outlines the cutwork area. A color stop will stop your embroidery sewing machine. Do not change thread color. The color stop is inserted only to allow you to cut out the fabric inside the cutwork areas.

b. When the stitching stops, remove the hoop from your embroidery sewing machine, but *do not remove the fabric from the hoop.*

c. Trim the fabric layer only, inside and close to the straight stitching outline but *do not trim the wash away stabilizer.* A pair of 4″ curved embroidery scissors is essential.

d. Put the hoop back into position onto your embroidery sewing machine and continue stitching. Richelieu bars are stitched in the cutout area. A satin stitch outline is stitched to cover the raw edges. Finally, the remainder of the design stitches out.

e. When the design is complete, remove from hoop. Trim away all thread tails from the front and the back of the design. Hold under running water to remove the wash away stabilizer. Wash, rinse and dry. While still damp spray with starch, let dry slightly and press.

APPLIQUÉ EMBROIDERY

a. Hoop background fabric and stabilizer. Put the hoop into position onto your embroidery sewing machine. Stitch out the first color in the design. This marks out the appliqué area with a straight stitch. A color stop will stop your embroidery sewing machine. Do not change thread color. The color stop is inserted only to allow you to place the appliqué fabric into position in the embroidery hoop.

b. Spray the back of a square of cotton print with temporary adhesive spray and lay over the appliqué area, making sure it covers the entire area.

c. Stitch the next color. This outlines the shape and holds the appliqué fabric in place with a straight stitch. A color stop will stop your embroidery sewing machine. Do not change thread color. The color stop is inserted only to allow you to trim away the excess appliqué fabric.

d. Once the stitching stops, remove the hoop from your embroidery sewing machine but *do not remove the fabric from the hoop.* Trim away the excess fabric close to the straight stitching outline.

e. Put the hoop back into position onto your embroidery sewing machine and stitch out the next color. A satin stitch outlines the appliqué, covering the raw edge. Stitch out the remaining colors to complete the design.

f. When the design is complete, remove from hoop. Trim away all thread tails from the front and the back of the design.

supply information

4" curved embroidery scissors feature a curved point that allows comfortable hand positioning in the embroidery hoop. The sharp points are fine enough for lace, cutwork, appliqué, tailoring and hand needlework.

40 wt rayon thread A lustrous thread used for decorative stitching such as machine embroidery, satin stitch appliqué, etc. 40 wt. rayon thread has an extensive color range and is well suited to most programmed embroidery. If your design is reversible you can also use 40 wt rayon in the bobbin.

Heirloom cotton thread This very fine 100% cotton thread is most often used with wing needle stitching where it must blend into the background fabric to allow an openwork effect to occur, such as hemstitching. Heirloom cotton thread is also a good choice for embroidery bobbin thread.

Cotton sewing thread Mercerized cotton thread is good for all general sewing.

Embroidery bobbin thread A very fine thread is required in the bobbin when doing hooped machine embroidery and various other decorative sewing techniques. We have used a wide variety of thread in cotton and polyester with good results. Choose one that works best for your machine. Consult your sewing machine retailer.

Eyelet cutter and mat A tool set that is used to punch out the fabric of an embroidery design to help create an eyelet.

Fade away marker While a variety of markers are available to mark sewing details on your fabric to make sewing easier, we generally prefer fade away markers. The markings disappear quickly and easily without having to launder the project.

Linen or linen/cotton blend fabric Our #1 choice for embroidery projects. Natural fibre fabrics such as cotton and linen lend themselves well to embroidery. They are more stable and tend to have a smoother surface texture.

Tear away stabilizer A material used to support fabric during decorative stitching to keep it from becoming distorted. After the decorative stitching has been completed, the stabilizer is removed by tearing it away. It is available in a variety of weights.

Temporary adhesive spray A spray on material that is used to secure fabric and/or stabilizer layers together so as to avoid slippage while stitching.

Seam sealant A liquid adhesive that keeps threads from raveling and fabric edges from fraying.

Spray on starch A convenient starch which is sprayed onto fabric and then ironed dry. Gives a crisp look to shirts, blouses and home linens.

Wash away stabilizer A water soluble material used to support fabric during decorative stitching to keep it from becoming distorted. After the decorative stitching has been completed, the stabilizer is removed by rinsing well with water. It is available in a variety weights and types.

Wing needle Is used for decorative stitching on woven fabric. The "wing" spreads fibres to create an openwork effect such as hemstitching on table linens.

notes

cd enclosure

Your purchase of this book includes a CD containing additional digital content. If the CD has been removed from the book, please do not purchase the book.

How to use this CD

Insert the CD into your computer's CD drive. Double click the *My Computer* icon on your computer's desktop. Double click on the *CD Drive* icon that you placed the CD into. Double click the *read_me.txt* icon. This will launch your computer's text program so that you can view the read_me.txt file. The *read_me.txt* file describes and explains how to access the files on your CD.

Copyright Information

By using the contents of this CD, you agree to the following: Snez Babic and Janice Wray hold the copyrights to all embroidery designs, project instructions and reference documents on the enclosed CD. They are for your personal use only. In accordance with copyright law, you may not copy, rent, lease, lend or modify in all or in part, using any media, any of the embroidery designs, project instructions or reference documents. However, you may display, sell, or give as gifts items made using these designs and instructions.

IMPORTANT: IF YOUR EMBROIDERY FIELD IS AT LEAST 5" X 9"

To stitch all of the Napkin Wrap designs on this CD, your embroidery field must be at least 6" x 9 1/2". However, some of the Napkin Wrap designs will fit an embroidery field that is at least 5" x 9", and therefore you can use them. Revised versions of the others, which have been edited to fit your embroidery field, are available to download from our web site at www.napkin-wraps.com (click on "Technical Info"). Your purchase of this book entitles you to download them to your computer. All other designs on the CD will fit in a 4" x 4" embroidery field.
